CRAYOLA ART OF COLOR

Mari Schuh

Lerner Publications ◆ Minneapolis

TO THE MARTIN COUNTY LIBRARY

Official Licensed Product
Lerner Publications Company
A division of Lerner Publishing Group, Inc.
241 First Avenue North
Minneapolis, MN 55401 USA

For reading levels and more information, look up this title at www.lernerbooks.com.

Main body text set in Billy Infant Regular 24/40.
Typeface provided by SparkyType.

Library of Congress Cataloging-in-Publication Data

Names: Schuh, Mari C., 1975– author.
Title: Crayola art of color / by Mari Schuh.
Description: Minneapolis : Lerner Publications, 2018. | Series: Crayola colorology | Includes bibliographical references and index. | Audience: Ages 4–9. | Audience: K to Grade 3.
Identifiers: LCCN 2017009606 (print) | LCCN 2017019213 (ebook) | ISBN 9781512497724 (eb pdf) | ISBN 9781512466881 (lb : alk. paper)
Subjects: LCSH: Color in art—Juvenile literature.
Classification: LCC ND1490 (print) | LCC ND1490 .S29 2018 (ebook) | DDC 752—dc23

LC record available at https://lccn.loc.gov/2017009606

Manufactured in the United States of America
1-43079-32453-6/16/2017

TABLE OF CONTENTS

Bursting with Color 4

Color and Feeling. 6

Light and Shadows. 12

Bold and Bright 18

Colors in Nature 24

Many Colors 28
Glossary. 30
To Learn More 31
Index. 32

BURSTING WITH COLOR

Bright red, pale blue, and grassy green.

Art is bursting with color!

Artists use color to tell stories.

The colors they use make us feel different emotions.

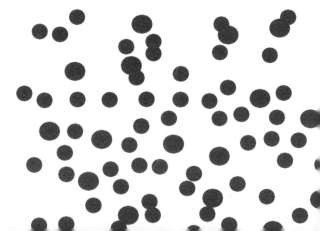

COLOR AND FEELING

Yellow,

orange,

and gold.

These bright, warm colors can make us feel happy.

Sunflowers, Vincent Van Gogh, 1888

This painting uses many soft colors.

Green is cool and calm.

The Japanese Footbridge, Claude Monet, 1899

The woman's dress is beautiful shades of gold.

Why do you think her dress is gold?

Portrait of Adele Bloch-Bauer I, Gustav Klimt, 1907

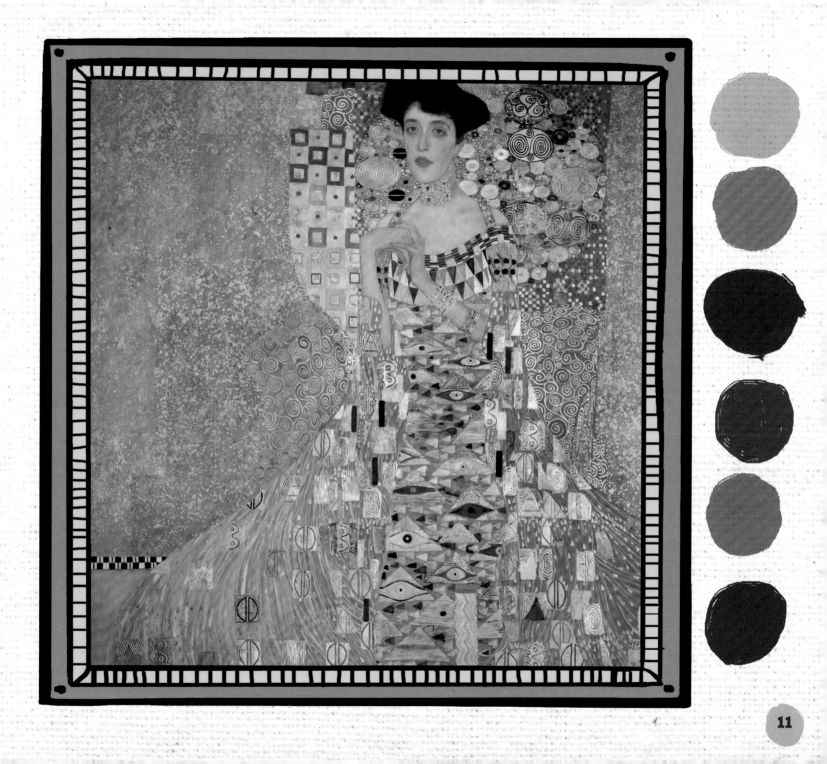

LIGHT AND SHADOWS

Light colors stand out against dark colors.

What's the first thing you see in this painting?

Girl with a Pearl Earring, Johannes Vermeer, 1665

13

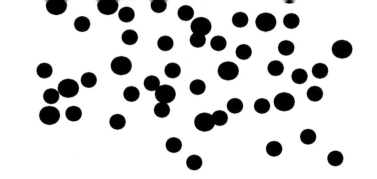

A day in the park was made with tiny dots of paint. Some places are sunny. Some places are shady.

Artists use dark colors to create shadows.

A Sunday on La Grande Jatte, Georges Seurat, 1884

See the shades of yellow and blue.

How many yellows and blues can you find?

The Boating Party, Mary Cassatt, 1893–1894

BOLD AND BRIGHT

Look at all the bold, bright colors!

Count all the colors you see.

Flight of an Aeroplane, Olga Vladimirovna Rozanova, 1916

19

Sometimes artists make paintings using only a few colors.

Artistic Architectonics, Lyubov Sergeevna Popova, 1916

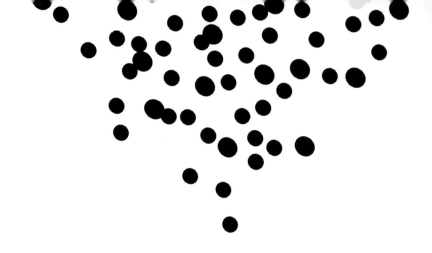

The reds, whites, and blues make your eyes move around this picture.

What else is made of red, white, and blue?

The 1920's . . . The Migrants Arrive and Cast Their Ballots,
Jacob Lawrence, 1974

COLORS IN NATURE

See the big green leaves.

Where might this woman be?

How can you tell?

Self Portrait with Monkey, Frida Kahlo, 1938

Look at the colors in the sky and in the waves.

The colors make a dark storm.

What else can colors tell you?

The Great Wave off Kanagawa, Katsushika Hokusai, 1831

MANY COLORS

The world is filled with so many colors. Here are some of the Crayola® crayon colors used in this book.

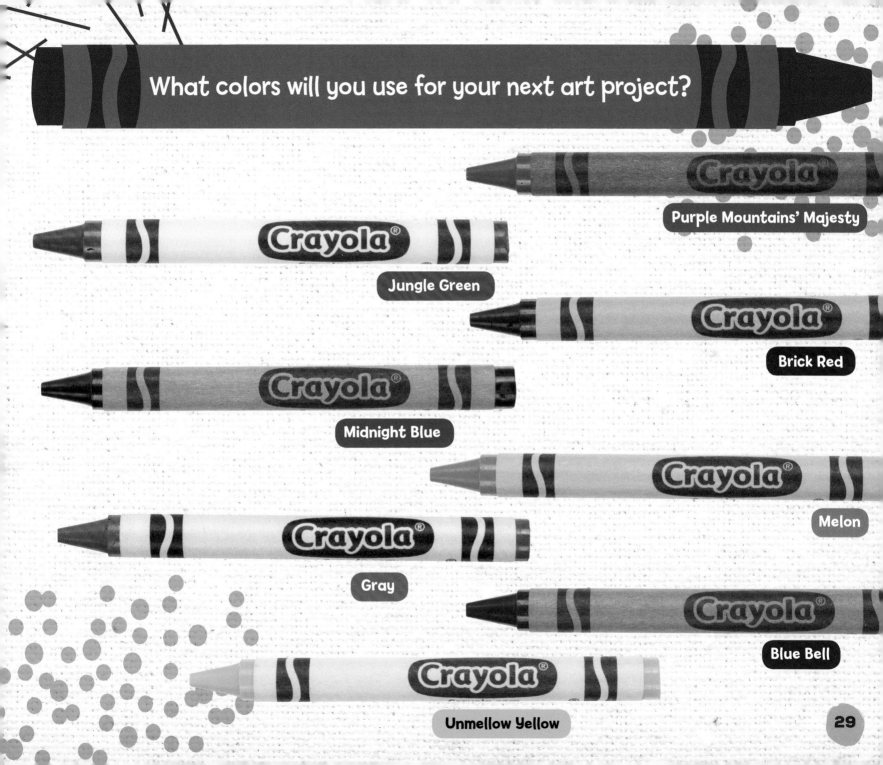

What colors will you use for your next art project?

Purple Mountains' Majesty

Jungle Green

Brick Red

Midnight Blue

Melon

Gray

Blue Bell

Unmellow Yellow

29

GLOSSARY

artists: people who make art, such as paintings, sculptures, and music

bold: able to stand out very clearly

calm: peaceful

emotions: strong feelings. Happiness, sadness, and anger are emotions.

mural: a painting on a wall or building

pale: having a light color

shades: the degrees of lightness or darkness of a color

shadows: shaded areas made when light is blocked

TO LEARN MORE

BOOKS

Blevins, Wiley. *Colors All Around*. South Egremont, MA: Red Chair, 2016.
  Read this book about a young girl discovering all the colors around her.

Cantillo, Oscar. *Green around Me*. New York: Cavendish Square, 2015.
  Discover all the places you can find the color green.

Osburn, Mary Rose. *I Know Colors*. New York: Gareth Stevens, 2017.
  Explore color by reading about common objects you might see every day.

WEBSITES

Cézanne's Astonishing Apples
  http://www.metmuseum.org/content/interactives/cezannes_apples/index.html
  Learn about a famous French artist who was known for painting apples.

Crayons with Paint
  http://www.crayola.com/things-to-do/how-to-landing/crayons-with-paint.aspx
  Try making some of your own art using crayons and paint.

INDEX

bright, 4, 6, 18

gold, 6, 10

green, 4, 8, 24

shades, 10, 16

shadows, 14

yellow, 6, 16

PHOTO ACKNOWLEDGMENTS

The images in this book are used with the permission of: © iStockphoto.com/kosmos111, p. 5; © RoyStudioEU/Shutterstock.com (linen background throughout); The National Gallery, London/Wikimedia Commons (CC 1.0 PDM), p. 7; Gift of Victoria Nebeker Coberly, in memory of her son John W. Mudd, and Walter H. and Leonore Annenberg, Image courtesy of the Board of Trustees, National Gallery of Art, Washington DC, p. 9; GalleriX/Wikimedia Commons (CC 1.0 PDM), p. 11; Mauritshuis/Wikimedia Commons (CC 1.0 PDM), p. 13; Art Institute of Chicago/Wikimedia Commons (CC 1.0 PDM), p. 15; Chester Dale Collection, Image courtesy of the Board of Trustees, National Gallery of Art, Washington DC, p. 17; © Art Museum, Samara, Russia/Bridgeman Images, p. 19; © Private Collection/Bridgeman Images, p. 21; © 2017 The Jacob and Gwendolyn Knight Lawrence Foundation, Seattle/Artists Rights Society (ARS), New York, image via © San Diego Museum of Art, USA; Gift of Lorillard, a Division of Loews Theatres, Inc./Bridgeman Images, p. 23; © 2017 Banco de México Diego Rivera Frida Kahlo Museums Trust, Mexico, D.F./Artists Rights Society (ARS), New York, image via © Albright-Knox Art Gallery/Art Resource, NY, p. 25; © The Stapleton Collection/Bridgeman Images, p. 27.

Cover: © Museum of Modern Art, New York, USA/Bridgeman Images (Starry Night); Wikimedia Commons (CC 1.0 PDM) (Mona Lisa); Antonov Roman/Shutterstock.com (right, framed oil-painting); RoyStudioEU/Shutterstock.com (linen texture background); TairA/Shutterstock.com (watercolor background).

LERNER

SOURCE

Expand learning beyond the printed book. Download free, complementary educational resources for this book from our website, www.lernerresource.com.